MW00723504

To:

_____

May you feel the
warm rays of God's hope
in your heart this very day!

From:

_____

Requests for information should be addressed to:
Inspirio, The gift group of Zondervan
Grand Rapids, Michigan 49530
http://www.inspiriogifts.com

Associate Editor and Project Manager: Janice Jacobson
Design Manager: Amy J. Wenger
Design: Kris Nelson
Editor: Molly C. Detweiler
Digital File Preparation: Donna Look

Printed in China

02 03 04/ HK / 5 4 3 2 1

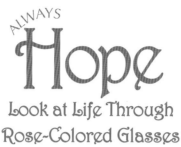

ALWAYS Hope

Look at Life Through
Rose-Colored Glasses

Written by Jody Houghton
WITH DORIS RIKKERS
Illustrated by Jody Houghton

inspirio.

Did you realize
that the sun
is always
shining?

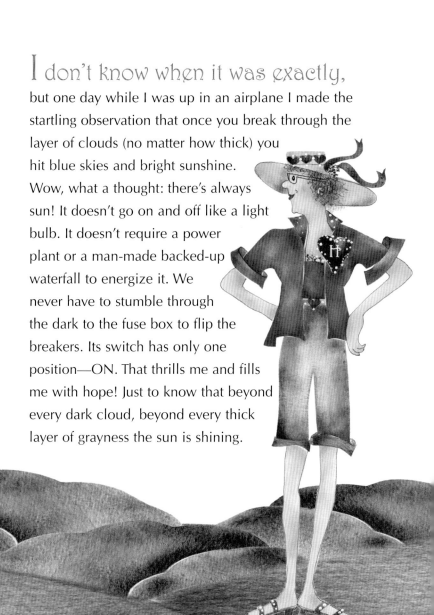

I don't know when it was exactly,

but one day while I was up in an airplane I made the startling observation that once you break through the layer of clouds (no matter how thick) you hit blue skies and bright sunshine. Wow, what a thought: there's always sun! It doesn't go on and off like a light bulb. It doesn't require a power plant or a man-made backed-up waterfall to energize it. We never have to stumble through the dark to the fuse box to flip the breakers. Its switch has only one position—ON. That thrills me and fills me with hope! Just to know that beyond every dark cloud, beyond every thick layer of grayness the sun is shining.

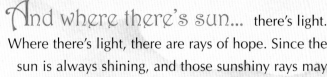

And where there's sun... there's light. Where there's light, there are rays of hope. Since the sun is always shining, and those sunshiny rays may come breaking through the clouds at any time I'm always prepared by wearing my rose-colored glasses. Do you like them? Faith and Charity gave them to me. They saw them in a shop at the beach and just had to buy them for me. They said that they both screamed my name when they saw this pair: "Oh, that is just like Hope, always looking at the world through rose-colored glasses! She's got to have these!"

6

I wear my glasses

to see the brighter side of life.
On days when I'm waiting
for the storm clouds to pass
over me and the sun to break
through, I enjoy viewing the
grayness through a mellow
pink hue. I always live in hope for the
rays of light to penetrate the clouds, to come
shining through and to break the heavens wide
open with warming rays of hope and God's love.

These glasses really work!
Would you like some?

Optimism

Ask God to help you see things from His perspective. Take one step after another. Before long, in spite of yourself, you may notice surprising signs of hope in your own backyard: the chuckle of a baby, the kindly light in a neighbor's eyes, the sweet kiss of a spouse, an undreamed-of opportunity.

BARBARA JOHNSON

Let us hold

unswervingly

to the hope

we profess,

for God

who promised

is faithful.

HEBREWS 10:23

"Good Morning!
Emmanuel Hospital. Hope speaking.
How may I direct your call?
Seventh floor nurses station …
yes, internal medicine. Your friend
had her gallbladder taken out?
Oh yes, my friend Faith did too.
One day in, one day out. She has no
problem with her tummy anymore.
You tell your friend to call us if
she would like a magazine or book.
The volunteer staff is always ready
to serve! I'll connect you.

And remember...
keep hope in your heart."

Emmanuel
Hospital
Volunteer

Hope
On Duty

Welcome

I love my job here at Emmanuel. I hear lots of stories and see lots of worried faces, but this is a hospital that lives up to its name. Emmanuel means "God is with us" and here at the hospital you can just feel his presence. How? Well, when someone is really sick here, the doctors never give up, they stay with the patient and do everything they can to restore their health. Many of the nurses here sit with frightened patients all night long, holding their hands and just being there. That's how God is with us and how he brings us hope, by working through his precious people!

It's a Girl

To:

Welcome

Oh, excuse me, here comes an excited and very happy lady!

"Well, hello there. I'm Hope. How may I help you?"

"I'm looking for the nursery. My daughter just had a baby– my first grandchild!"

"Well, congratulations! How thrilling for you. Boy or girl?"

"Oh, it's a little girl. She was born just a few hours ago. My daughter said she's the cutest little thing in the world!"

"The nursery is on the fourth floor. Take the elevators down the hall on your right. And give that new baby a kiss. Enjoy every minute of her."

"Oh, thank you, Hope. What a lovely name. New babies give us hope, too, don't they?!"

 "They certainly do. God renews our hope every time a new baby comes into the world—it reminds me that he's still here, giving us great gifts! Bye now... and God bless!"

God is With Us

Remember that the love of God

has no limits, no boundaries,

and no prejudices. No matter

who you are, where you are,

or where you've been,

he loves you.

He holds you; he carries you;

he remains with you at all times.

MARILYN MEBERG

God has said,
"Never will I
leave you;
never will
I forsake you."

HEBREWS 13:5

$\mathcal{C}$very morning I start my day with a refreshing shower. Some days I'm in such a hurry, I just jump in, grab the soap and shampoo, rinse off and jump out. Other times, when I'm thinking about a situation in my life, or maybe when I'm still sleepy from a restless night, I move a little slower.

This morning, I'm taking my time. I've got some serious decisions to make today, and I've got a lot on my mind. As I reached for the shampoo, I noticed the label, "A mild everyday shampoo that provides gentle cleansing without any build-up, irritation to the scalp, or damage to your hair—Wet hair thoroughly, Apply, lather, and rinse. Follow with conditioner. Ph Balanced."

With these simple instructions in mind, my routine shower became a nurturing gift to myself—"a gentle cleansing" of my mind, "without any build-up" of unresolved problems; "no irritation" because God's peace is in my heart; and "no damage" because God is flooding hope into my soul and soothing all my worries away.

I let the warm water drown all my concerns and then, as I shape a bubble crown of shampoo on my head, I begin humming a tune. Suddenly my ordinary routine has turned into a Sensational Shower of Blessings! My head clears as the water rinses away the shampoo. Solutions to my challenges present themselves. Once again I know what God wants me to do.

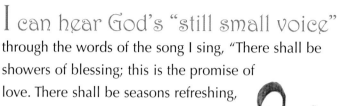

I can hear God's "still small voice" through the words of the song I sing, "There shall be showers of blessing; this is the promise of love. There shall be seasons refreshing, sent from the Savior above."

As I wrap my body in a clean fresh towel, I'm ready for this brand new day, assured that God's promises and blessings will guide me along my way. I am conditioned and balanced and hope-freshened in a bright new way!

There shall be
showers of blessing,
If we but trust
and obey;
There shall be
seasons refreshing,
If we let God
have His way.

DANIEL W. WHITTLE

"I will send down
showers in season;
there will be
showers of blessing,"
says the Lord.

EZEKIEL 34:26

Years ago when I was a little girl, my Grandmother Harmony gave me this beautiful rosewood hope chest. "Every girl needs a hope chest," she said. "Keep your most prized possessions in it. Fill it with reminders that will always give you hope."

And just as she advised, I keep some very special things in my hope chest, like this set of six rose-colored glass dessert plates and matching glasses. They're from my grandmother. She would always bring them out of the china closet and invite my sisters and me over for raspberry lemonade and sugar cookies, just to bring a little hope and joy into our lives. "Hope is what helps us always have joy," she would say, "so it's always best to stop focusing on yourself. Focus on something else and someone else.

When you're giving hope to others it's impossible not to get filled up with it yourself!" Sure enough her little pink parties always put a smile on our faces and they perked up her spirits too.

Ever since those childhood days,

I've been collecting reminders to help me see the good in life, things that will always give me hope—recordings of songs that mark a special time in my life, some spiritually uplifting, some that just put a smile on my face; a pressed flower blossom from the backyard of my childhood home; sand in a little jar from a vacation long ago—all the little things that fill life with hope, mixed in my chest with the treasured dishes and handmade doilies.

Just lifting the lid of my rosewood chest, reminds me of the blessings in my life and God's great promises for the future. Long, long, ago someone engraved the words "Always Hope" on the lid of my treasure box, and I am thankful that long ago, God etched "Always Hope" on my heart.

Always Hope

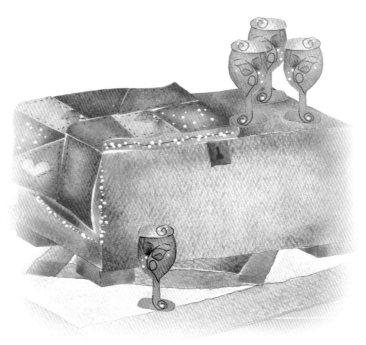

All the lovely memories
That God has given me
Help me to remember
That there are more to be.

MOLLY DETWEILER

The best and most
beautiful things in the world
cannot be seen or even touched—
they must be felt with the heart.

HELEN KELLER

I will always
have hope;
I will praise you
more and more, Lord.

PSALM 71:14

My mother, my grandmother, and her mother before her all used this one little poem to help get them going in the mornings. It was their formula for brushing away the "sleepies" and I've inherited it as my own:

When the going gets tough

And there's no hope to be found,

Clean something,

arrange something,

Or just move things around!

The words "clean," "arrange," and "move" are the top three items that I place on a To Do List. Just writing those words is the beginning of action that scoops me up, gives me energy, and gets me moving.

I was having a bit of a tough day just yesterday. Nothing seemed to go quite right! I remembered that old saying, went straight to the closet and got out the Hoover. Action was required! Clean something, arrange something, tackle the junk drawer! Does the refrigerator need to be cleaned out? This is a great formula for moving those rough days out the door and into the trash where they belong!

Suck it up! Throw it out! Just thinking about it makes me feel better.

Life is
Good

Vacuuming works best for me.

I really put my shoulder into it—click the setting to "Full Power"—out, back, out, back. I work the pattern in my carpet so every inch is covered. The "vrooooom" sound drowns out the noisy world. Before long I get into the rhythm of my work and start feeling the sense of accomplishment that only comes from doing a project that makes things better than the way they were before. I've even forgotten what it was that sent me to the Hoover with such on-the-job-passion in the first place!

So get moving. The Lord will provide the energy. Motion gives you energy, energy produces movement, and movement, purpose. Take it one task at a time. God didn't make the world in a day, he took six days: one step, one task at a time. He even took the time to step back, check out his work, and declare it good.

Sometimes when you get moving, even on the smallest task, you suddenly have a purpose—you see everything organized and cleaned up—and you're ready to handle the next project with ease and grace … and hope! Don't forget to step back, check out your work as you close the closet door and declare: Life is good!

Life is Good

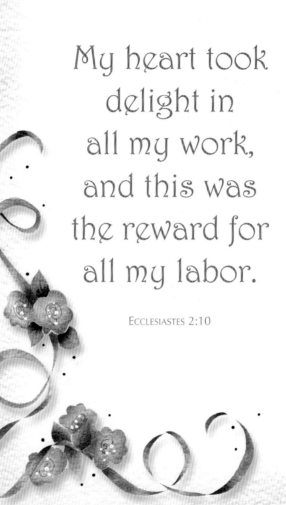

My heart took
delight in
all my work,
and this was
the reward for
all my labor.

ECCLESIASTES 2:10

FAITH

makes all things possible.

LOVE

makes all things easy.

HOPE

makes all things work.

I'm the first of my friends to declare,
"It's Thrift Store Shopping Day"!

The Goodwill and Salvation Army stores are full of wonderful surprises!

But a lot of times Faith and Charity aren't as optimistic as I am about finding a really good treasure. I'm always convinced that we'll be successful in finding a replacement lid to my old avocado green saucepan, or a crystal goblet to add to Charity's treasured cut glass collection, or a gravy boat to match Faith's discontinued lavender floral china pattern.

THRIFT STORE

Everyone Welcome

It's a treasure hunt for me... among shelves and tables full of kitchenware, looking for one special size, one certain color, I'm always keeping hope in my heart. I walk up and down the aisles, lifting plate after plate, searching in dark corners and on high shelves. "I can never find what I'm really looking for," Faith sighs, "and I end up with more things than I really need, but … don't you just love this little tea pot? It would be perfect for our next tea party!"

"Only you, Hope, can find a true gem, the exact fit, or color—you just keep hanging in there," Charity smiles. "You're persistent enough to dig through mountains of boxes and rows and rows of shelves of those mismatched pots and pans, cups, and glasses. You're an expert treasure hunter, Hope!"

"**Well**," I always say, "you've got to
be optimistic, you have to have hope.
There's the perfect something out there, you just have to
keep looking. I guess it's kind of like life … you need to
always keep hope in your heart as you
travel from day to day, seeking God's
perfect gifts and his wonderful plan.
One day you'll find it in the most
unexpected spot, just waiting
there for you to unveil its
hiding place!"

Store up for yourselves
treasures in heaven ...
for where your treasure is,
there your heart will be also.

MATTHEW 6:20–21

Do not be afraid,
little flock,
for our Father
has been pleased
to give you the kingdom.

LUKE 12:32

Riches I heed not,
nor man's empty praise,
Thou mine Inheritance,
now and always:
Thou and Thou only,
first in my heart,
High King of heaven,
my Treasure Thou art.

TRANSLATED BY MARY E. BYRNE

I have a confession to make. I'm a morning person.

Mornings to me are the most special time of day. And my little bird, Buttercup, agrees with me 100 percent. Each morning, when I get up, I enter the kitchen and remove the tea towel from over Buttercup's cage.

"Good morning, Buttercup!" I announce cheerfully, shaking out the towel covered with the little yellow flowers that match my birdie's name. Without fail, my little yellow Buttercup, chirps a happy hello. Even in the earliest morning hour, when the sun is still struggling to creep over the horizon, Buttercup will twitter and tweet a happy, welcome-morning song to me. She's already up, hopping from perch to perch, eager for some fresh water and a serving of seeds.

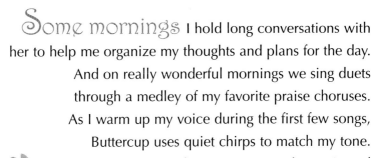

Some mornings I hold long conversations with her to help me organize my thoughts and plans for the day. And on really wonderful mornings we sing duets through a medley of my favorite praise choruses. As I warm up my voice during the first few songs, Buttercup uses quiet chirps to match my tone. But as I become more enthusiastic and sing at the top of my voice, Buttercup displays the fullness of her birdsong and lets out trills with her most complex chirps and tweets. Her collection of songs doesn't end with the morning hit-parade. She sings in the afternoons, at twilight, and at night fall. Without fail, my happy little bird is always singing a happy, hopeful song.

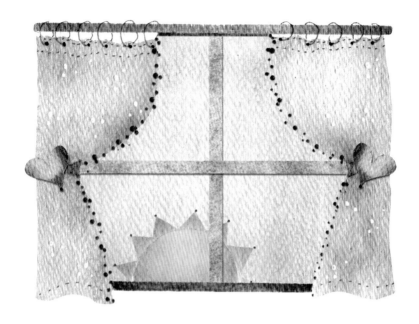

Buttercup is my little burst of sunshine

even on a cold and dreary winter morning. She reminds me that worry is a waste of time, and that singing a happy song gives hope and lifts the spirit. Starting the day with a Buttercup song and my sunshine mug filled with coffee, lifts my spirits and invigorates me to start a new day.

Satisfy us in the morning

with your unfailing love,

O Lord,

that we may sing

for joy and be glad

all our days.

<small>PSALM 90:14</small>

"Hope"

is the thing with feathers—

That perches in the soul—

And sings the tune

without the words—

And never stops—at all.

EMILY DICKINSON

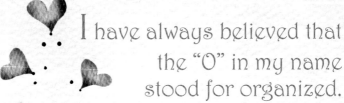

I have always believed that the "O" in my name stood for organized.

All my life I've been the one with the neatest room. When my friends wanted to play outside, I wanted to organize my closet—rearrange my dolls and neatly sort their clothes and accessories into shoeboxes with bright labels on each end. I was the one who painted parking spaces on the garage floor so my sisters and I could neatly put our bikes in a row every night. And whenever my mother asked, I was more than willing to help rearrange the spice cabinet's collection of little tins and boxes.

Today I still enjoy organizing things—the books in the bookcase, the office supplies in my desk drawer, the canceled checks from my checkbook, the receipts and how-to manuals and guarantee forms from my appliances. Being organized gives me peace of mind. But most of all, it frees me up to help others.

Today's "To-Do" List

4:00
Bus

Milk
Eggs
Butter

Always
Hope

Love

Faith
and
Charity
7:00
Tonight

Staying organized keeps me hopeful–hopeful
that I'll find what I need when I need it; hopeful that I'll
not waste time; hopeful that with added time (from not
searching for things and getting frustrated about it) I will
remain full of hope and energy to help someone else.

Why, just the other day

the perfect opportunity arose. My neighbor, Joy, called me on the phone, "Hope, I know how busy you are, but I really need a favor."

"No problem," I said.

"I have a doctor's appointment this afternoon, and I'm not sure how long it will take. So I might not be here when my boys get off the school bus. Would you be a dear and be at the house to welcome them home?"

"Oh sure thing, " I said enthusiastically. "What time?" I looked at my afternoon list again— it was filled with things to do. *Oh well,* I said to myself, *these will just have to go! Milk and cookies and a warm smile for little boys is more important than accomplishing a bunch of stuff. If I rearrange my morning, stay focused and organized, perhaps I can get everything done before the school bus arrives with the boys.*

With my mission in mind, I went into action and, wouldn't you know it, I got everything accomplished and I was waiting on the porch steps at 3:40 just as the school bus arrived and deposited the two grinning little boys.

I often get teased about being so organized. But it's times like these that I realize God gave me a special gift I can share with others–hope! It's not just an idiosyncrasy of mine, it's a treasure from God!

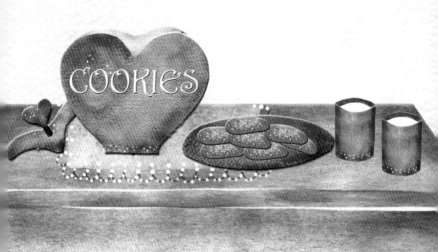

If we sit down at set of sun

And count the acts that we have done,

And, counting, find

One self-denying act, one word

That eased the heart of him who heard

One glance most kind

That fell like sunshine where it went

Then we may count that day well spent.

AUTHOR UNKNOWN

Do not forget
to do good
and to share with others,
for with such sacrifices
God is pleased.

HEBREWS 13:16

The night ahead promised to be perfect—warm, with a soft wind blowing and the fresh scent of lilac in the air.

I called my friends Charity and Faith just as it was growing dark. "Come over," I said. "It's warm and I have fresh, luscious strawberries with ice cream."

"But it's too hot to move," Faith complained.

"I just finished dinner," Charity sighed.

"No excuses. Come as you are. Just trust me. There is always room for ice cream."

It was the height of summer—the crickets sang and the tree frogs chirped as we gathered on the front porch enjoying our sweet strawberries and ice cream.

"Sit down and be still for a few minutes," I encouraged them, "and watch the meadow." (I have a marvelous, natural garden next door to me. Well, it's really a vacant lot, but over the years it has become a wild garden of native flowers: Queen Anne's lace, blue chicory, golden rod, and tall grasses with wheat-like tassely tops.)

"Are you going to tell us what we're watching for?" Charity asked.

"You'll see for yourself very soon. Just watch."

Within minutes it started to happen.

As the bugs hovered over the field, first one, than another flashed a little light—blink, blink, blink-blink. Soon the air over the meadow was full of sparkling, twinkling light, creating a glittering, glorious effect in the warm summer night. Little blinks came from everywhere. Twinkling bits of light flashed simultaneously and alternately. They blinked so fast you couldn't really see where they were coming from.

"Oh, look!" Charity exclaimed. "It's like Christmas! All those twinkling little lights! How magnificent!"

"Why didn't I ever notice them before?" Faith wondered.

"Sometimes you have to sit, watch, and listen to capture the small details of God's creation," I told them.

"Only you, Hope, would notice the little things— those little details that can make the end of a day so joyful," reflected Charity.

How many
are your works,
O Lord!
In wisdom
you made them all;
the earth is full
of your creatures.

Psalm 104:24

For the beauty
of each hour,
Of the day and
of the night,
Hill and vale,
and tree and flower,
Sun and moon,
and stars of light.
Lord of all,
to Thee we raise,
This our hymn
of grateful praise.

FOLLIOT S. PIERPOINT

It was my birthday last week.

Can you believe it … it was the big five-o! I just kept thinking, *My mom should be having this birthday, not me!* I used to think that people were getting really old when they turned fifty. Hmmm … I think I've had a change of heart about that! Well, even, me, Hope, whose motto is "There's Always Hope," was feeling a bit blue about heading into my fifth decade. But with friends like Faith and Charity, you can't be blue for long.

Just as I was finishing a second bowl of Triple Chocolate Fudge ice cream and feeling really sorry for myself, the phone rang. "Hope, you must come to my house right now." It was Charity and I could tell that something was up by the barely restrained giggle in her voice. So, I shook myself out of my chocolate-induced daze and headed on over.

Everything seemed awfully quiet as I walked up Charity's sidewalk. But as I opened the door I was met with a shout of "surprise" and an incredible explosion of PINK! My dear friends Hope and Charity had created a Pink Party, just for me! Those birthday blues flew out the window as I was enveloped in a rosy room full of warm wishes.

The guests were all wearing pink—and not just tasteful pink sweaters, oh no—everyone had been creatively extravagant about wearing pink. Oh, the screams of laughter we had over all the pink boas, hot pink shoes, and tiaras of pink rhinestones. Pink prom dresses came out of the back of several closets. It was fabulous! Plus, wonderful party favors were given to everyone—rose-colored sunglasses just like mine!

That evening we all shared stories of times when we were "in the pink." We ate a strawberry pink ice cream cake with "Happy Birthday, Hope" written on it in pink sprinkles. Sparkly pink heart confetti was everywhere! What a great celebration!

Even the most optimistic folks sometimes get the blues. That's when God turns our world rosy with the love of good friends. I love that about him!

Fabulous
50

A friend
knows the
song in my heart
and sings it to me
when my memory fails.

DONNA ROBERTS

A happy heart
makes the face
cheerful....
A cheerful heart
has a continual
feast.

PROVERBS 15:13, 15

Meet Hope's friends Faith & Charity

in their own special books. Also look for matching magnetic notepads and Postcard Daybreaks!

Everyday Faith
Walk with God and
You'll Never Be Out of Step
ISBN: 0-310-98570-6

Abiding Charity
God Loves You Just
the Way You Are!
ISBN: 0-310-98812-8